HISTORY OF
SCOTLAND

Colin Baxter

Colin Baxter Photography, Grantown-on-Spey, Scotland

History of Scotland

Scotland is replete with its own history. People have lived here for probably 10,000 years, each group leaving its mark on what came before. For some the evidence is sparse, perhaps because they used perishable materials, perhaps because there were few of them, perhaps because their work has been taken and reworked by later hands. But everywhere the tangle of history overlays itself with the passage of time.

These photographs entice you to discover more about those fascinating places and stories, leading you into a selection of places which have been built, destroyed or created through the ages by people in Scotland.

Scotland's heroes are also set into the context of their time and place: William Wallace, 'Guardian of Scotland' and victor at Stirling Bridge in 1297; King Robert the Bruce, chiefly remembered for his victory at Bannockburn; Rob Roy MacGregor, outlaw of the Trossachs; Charles Rennie Mackintosh, sadly under-appreciated in his own time…

Broadly in chronological order, this book enables you to follow threads through the weave of Scotland's history, from the intriguing settlements and megaliths of prehistory, through the fascinating Dark Ages and the establishment of the great cathedrals and castles, and finally, into the later monuments to Scotland's remarkable industrial heritage. Here is a sample of some of the best moments from Scotland's historic past.

◀ SKARA BRAE VILLAGE, ORKNEY

The most perfect Neolithic or Stone Age village in Europe, a remarkable window to the past. Preserved for centuries beneath windblown sand, here is the evidence of a lifestyle from 5000 years ago: fully furnished houses with hearths, benches, shelves, dressers and beds, all fashioned from stone. There were decorated jars, whale-bone dishes, beads, pins and pendants and heather mattresses with furs and skins for bedding. With a varied diet harvested from land and sea, these early people were not so different from us.

STONES OF STENNESS, ORKNEY

Piercing skywards out of the flat Orcadian landscape, these three enigmatic stones were important to our forebears. About 300 BC there was a complete stone circle here. Scotland's many standing stones or megaliths remain a mystery but, so often set-out in remarkably precise mathematical forms, they surely represent some sort of spiritual expression.

Iona Abbey Church

The island of Iona has been Scotland's most hallowed place of pilgrimage for more than 15 centuries. Today the restored 13th-century Benedictine abbey stands near the site of St Columba's 6th-century monastery – founded in 563 after he was banished from Ireland. Despite destruction by Norse invaders Iona's community has survived and flourished.

Loch Affric, ▶ Inverness-shire

The 'Great Wood of Caledon' the Caledonian pine forest, once swathed the Highlands in a blanket of trees. Dominated by Scots pine, it was a mixed woodland forming a mosaic with lochans, bogs and mountain-tops. With clearance for settlement, cultivation and grazing, and the consumption of timber for a myriad of uses, the great 'wildwood' slowly perished. Today only fragments survive including some ancient pines; witnesses to more than 300 years of Scottish history.

JEDBURGH ABBEY, BORDERS – founded in the 12th century.

URQUHART CASTLE, LOCH NESS

The strategically important site of Urquhart Castle is rich in archaeological evidence of early settlements, including a vitrified Iron-Age fort, a 6th-century Pictish settlement and a Norman motte and bailey. The present ruinous castle was largely built in the 16th century. The castle was destroyed and rebuilt many times throughout its history.

◀ Caerlaverock Castle, Dumfries-shire

This unique triangular castle was first built about 1290 by the Maxwells. It was besieged and recaptured several times in its history, falling first to Edward I in 1300. It was soon regained by the Maxwells; similar exchanges occured until 1640 when it was finally captured and dismantled by Covenanters.

Wallace Monument, ▶ by Stirling

William Wallace is possibly Scotland's most famous patriot. Renowned for his victory over the English at Stirling Bridge in 1297, he became Guardian of Scotland. His successes enraged Edward I, and he died a brutal death in London, in the name of Scottish liberty.

◀ ROBERT THE BRUCE STATUE

King and hero. Ironically, he initially allied himself with England and was over 30 before fully committing to the Scottish cause. Enthroned as King of Scots in 1306 he was master of guerrilla warfare and political manoeuvring. He ensured Scotland's independence on the battlefield and against the opposition of Pope John XXII through the remarkable 'Declaration of Arbroath'.

STIRLING CASTLE ▶

Bannockburn, June 1314. The final battle in the 'Wars of Independence' was fought against the English for control of Stirling Castle. Despite the Scottish victory, Bruce ordered the destruction of the castle's defences to ensure it could not be held against him.

◀ St Andrews, Fife

Famed home of golf and earliest seat of learning. St Andrews Cathedral, the largest in the land, was complete by the end of the 13th century when the town's castle was already 100 years old. The University was founded in 1412. But the town's fortunes reversed with the Protestant Reformation (1560), which brought martyrdom, murder and destruction.

Edinburgh Castle ▶

Favoured royal residence for two centuries after the Wars of Independence, the castle was birthplace of Mary Queen of Scots' only son in 1566. In 1603 the crowns of Scotland and England were remarkably united when he, James VI of Scotland, succeeded to the English throne.

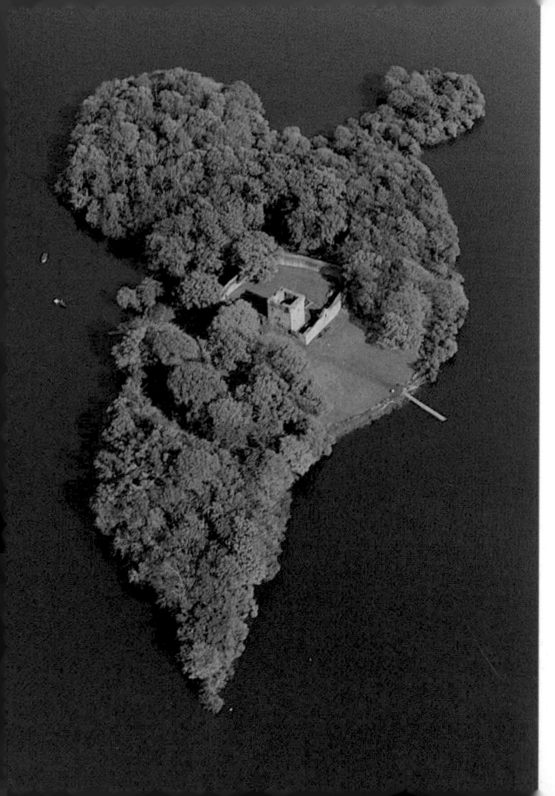

◀ LOCH LEVEN CASTLE, KINROSS

Island prison of Mary, Queen of Scots after her controversial marriage to the Earl of Bothwell, Loch Leven Castle was the stage for the final act of her reign. Here she was forced to abdicate in 1567 in favour of her infant son. She escaped, but later sealed her fate by asking Queen Elizabeth of England for protection.

THE RIVER GARRY ▶ AT KILLIECRANKIE, TAYSIDE

On 27 July 1689 the tranquillity of this now famous beauty spot was shattered by 2500 Jacobite Highlanders charging a government army double their number. Led by Viscount Dundee, who died that day, this Jacobite victory was one of few over the next 50 years.

GLENCOE, LOCHABER

A place of awesome beauty. A name which evokes images of bloodshed. For here, in February 1692, 38 MacDonalds of Glencoe were massacred by a force led by Campbell of Glenlyon, because their Clan chief had arrived late to swear loyalty to King William.

EILEAN DONAN CASTLE, LOCH DUICH

An ancient stronghold. During the 1719 Jacobite Rising it was bombarded by government frigates, and then systematically blown up. The stark ruins stood neglected for 200 years until it was restored between 1912 and 1932 by Colonel MacRae-Gilstrap.

◀ BEN VENUE & LOCH KATRINE

The splendour of the picturesque Trossachs around Loch Katrine, home to the Clan Gregor for many centuries, only came to the notice of the outside world in the 19th century. Much admired by William and Dorothy Wordsworth on their tour with Samuel Coleridge in 1803, its enduring fame was ensured by Walter Scott's 1810 poem *The Lady of the Lake*. In its time, the poem was a literary sensation which inspired streams of visitors to travel north to explore the romantic landscapes.

ROB ROY'S GRAVE, BALQUHIDDER

Villain or hero? Probably both. An outlawed cattle dealer, who turned to 'blackmail' – protection of cattle in return for payment – and deeds of daring. He led Clan Gregor for the Jacobites at Sheriffmuir (1715) but may have spied for the Government. He died a free man, aged 62, in 1734 and was buried at Balquhidder in his beloved Trossachs.

◀ Glenfinnan Monument & Loch Shiel, Lochaber

Here, on 19 August 1745, Prince Charles Edward Stewart, the charismatic 'Bonnie Prince', raised his standard at the beginning of the last Jacobite Rising. Since 1689 'Jacobites', the supporters of the dethroned James VII and later his son James 'the Old Pretender', had fought to regain the crown. The Rising which began at Glenfinnan ended disastrously at Culloden Moor on 16 April 1746.

Fort George, Moray Firth ▶

Built in response to the Jacobite Rising of 1745, Fort George is said to be the 'most regular fortification' in Britain. Designed to hold 1600 men, it took 24 years to complete (1747-70), cost over £150,000 and never witnessed a shot fired in anger.

PORTREE HARBOUR, ISLE OF SKYE

Port righ, King's Harbour. Named for James V who visited in 1540, but best known as the capital of Skye and for its connection with Bonnie Prince Charlie. For five months in 1746, after his defeat at Culloden, the Prince was a fugitive in the western Highlands and Islands. Disguised as 'Betty Burke', he was smuggled to Skye by Flora Macdonald. On parting in Portree, he gave her a gold locket containing his portrait.

QUEEN STREET DOORWAYS, EDINBURGH ▶

Doorways in one of the three principal streets of the New Town. Based on a gridiron plan, the New Town was designed by James Craig and begun in 1767.

48

◀ Finnieston Crane, Glasgow

A monument to Glasgow's industrial heritage. When it was built in the 1930s, it was the largest crane of its kind in Europe. Previously it hoisted steam locomotives from the Springburn Works onto ships which would carry their cargoes all over the globe. Today it stands as a relic of Glasgow's prowess in an era of engineering greatness.

The River Clyde ▶

Scotland's third largest river played an important part in Glasgow's development as a major industrial and trading centre from the 18th century onwards. Between 1810 and 1980 more than 30,000 ships were launched from over 80 Clyde yards. Names like John Brown's shipyard and great liners such as the *Queen Mary* are part of the Clyde's illustrious past.

◀ Forth Rail Bridge

When the railway bridge across the River Forth opened in 1890 it was the longest bridge, and largest steel structure, in the world. Its unique cantilever design contains 8 million rivets and 55,000 tons of steel, and 57 men died during its construction. It is also recorded that 8000 men's caps had been retrieved from the water below. Including its viaducts, the bridge is one mile and 1005 yards long and is still fully operational. Today it is recognised worldwide as a monument to Scottish engineering.

Glenfinnan Viaduct, West Highland Line

The first concrete viaduct, 1897-1901, with 21 standard spans. Built on the famously scenic West Highland Line, it marks the end of over a century of Scottish engineering unsurpassed in the world. Men like Thomas Telford and Joseph Mitchell had revolutionised communications with their roads, canals and bridges.

THE HILL HOUSE, HELENSBURGH (1902)

Designed by Charles Rennie Mackintosh, now regarded as one of Scotland's most talented architects, artists and designers, The Hill House was commissioned by Walter Blackie in 1902. Mackintosh was greatly under-appreciated in his own lifetime, despite his creative achievements which paved the way for the Modern Movement.

THE VILLAGE, ▶
ST KILDA

Truly utilitarian buildings at the heart of a self-sufficient community. For many centuries the people of St Kilda lived in isolation 110 miles from mainland Scotland. Their rents of feathers, oil and dried seabirds were collected annually for their MacLeod chief. But tourism, education, stern Presbyterianism and the ravages of tetanus combined to seal the community's fate. In 1930 the last 36 islanders petitioned the Government to be evacuated. Today the island is designated as a World Heritage Site.